Theology Today

5 The Theology of Creation

Theology Today

GENERAL EDITOR:
EDWARD YARNOLD, S.J.

No. 5

The Theology of Creation

BY

ROBERT BUTTERWORTH, S.J.

distributed by
CLERGY BOOK SERVICE
BUTLER, WISCONSIN

CONTENTS

ACKNOWLEDGEMENTS

The Scripture quotations in the publication are from the *Revised Standard Version of the Bible* copyrighted 1946 and 1952 by the Division of Christian Education of the National Council of the Churches of Christ in the U.S.A. and used by permission; the quotations from *The Documents of Vatican II* (ed. W. M. Abbott, S.J.) are printed by kind permission of the America Press and Geoffrey Chapman, London.

ABBREVIATIONS

Dz H. Denzinger & A. Schönmetzer,
    Enchiridion Symbolorum, Definitionum et
    Declarationum (33rd edit., Barcelona etc., 1965).

PREFACE

Creation is not only a doctrine of Christianity, but a Christian doctrine.

It is one of the truths contained in the Nicene Creed: '...one God, the almighty Father, maker of heaven and earth, maker of all things visible and invisible.' But that does not make it a specifically *Christian* truth. It can only be that if it allows a central role to Christ, 'through whom all things were made', as the Creed continues.

Fr Butterworth's purpose is to do this. He shows that God's action in creating the world is not distinct from his action for man's salvation. Both activities, therefore, must be through Christ. 'All things were created through him and for him... In him all the fulness of God was pleased to dwell, and through him to reconcile to himself all things' (Col 1.16-20). This was the vision of St. Paul and Teilhard.

E. J. Yarnold, S.J.

INTRODUCTION

This essay on the theology of creation tries to be true to its title. It is therefore likely that it will be of little or even no interest to some would-be readers. Anyone seeking simply an *aggiornamento* of familiar Church doctrine will not find it here. In fact, this essay springs from a certain dissatisfaction with the traditional Church teaching of creation. Again, anyone seeking light on cosmic origins will be very disappointed. It is not a theologian's job to peddle scientific lore about the mode or process of creation. And no theologian would try to give a blow-by-blow commentary on God's initial creative activity.

Rather, this essay sets out to present creation in an unusual guise – as a *Christian* truth. The Christian theologian's work is a work of interpretation. He must try to interpret, to translate into meaningful language – using whatever ways of thinking and speaking he finds most apt – that truth about God, about God's actions, about God's relationship with man and his world, which God himself reveals to men in his supreme self-revelation which is Jesus Christ. Basic revealed truth about God includes the relationship between the world and God which is founded on God's creation of that world, and of man in it. Creation and the ensuing relationship – which is constitutive not only of the fact *that* the world is but also of *what* the world is meant to be – is a revealed truth that must be interpreted by the theologian to believers, so that they can come to appreciate the religious *meaning* of it. The trouble is that little of this kind of interpretation has gone on with regard to the revealed truth of creation. Creation has too often been taken for granted. Little has been done to give the believer the religious cash-value of the truth. It is no exaggeration to say that, by and large, creation is not considered a *Christian* truth – truth to live a Christian life by.

So this essay tries to bring out the Christian meaning of creation: in other words, to outline the Christian theology of creation. In order to do this, it has seemed best to let the authentic record of God's self-revelation in Jesus Christ – the Scriptures – do most of the talking. It is from them that the theologian can get the best guidance concerning the way he must think and speak in his interpretation of the revealed Christian doctrine of creation.

CHAPTER 1

THE CHURCH'S DOCTRINE OF CREATION

It must be admitted that the Church's traditional teaching on the subject of creation, in so far as it has any place at all in the consciousness of the Catholic believer, is not always as enriching or life-enhancing a doctrine as it might fairly be expected to be. After all, the doctrine must surely be an attempt to express the fact of a relationship between God and his creation which can only be of the deepest significance and concern for anyone who really confesses belief 'in one God, the almighty Father, maker of heaven and earth, maker of all things, visible and invisible'. And yet the traditional doctrine of the Church somehow fails to form and support an abiding consciousness in the believer of the basic and vivid truth of the fact of God's continually creative relationship with everything that exists apart from himself. Why does the Church's traditional teaching fail to produce a proportionate effect? It is the purpose of this brief essay both to diagnose the fault and to suggest the remedy.

Vatican I on Creation

There are few official Church documents which embody the traditional doctrine on creation. Selection of them for quotation is made all the easier because a very comprehensive statement of the official faith in creation – in fact, a solemn and infallible definition – was issued by

13

the First Vatican Council in 1870:

> The Holy Catholic Apostolic Roman Church believes and confesses that there is one true and living God, *Creator and Lord of heaven and earth*, almighty, 'eternal, unmeasured, incomprehensible', infinite in mind and will and in every perfection. Since he is one, sole, 'utterly simple' and unalterable spiritual substance, he must be said to be *really and essentially distinct* from the world, supremely blessed in himself and of himself, and ineffably exalted above all the things which exist, or can be thought of, besides himself (Dz 3001).

> This sole, true God, of his goodness and 'almighty power' – not in order to increase or to acquire his own blessedness, but in order to show forth his perfection by means of the good things which he bestows on creatures – by a completely free decision '*established*, at the same time as time began, *creatures* of both kinds, spiritual and bodily (namely angelic and this-wordly), *from nothing*; and then the human creature, made up of spirit and body, as it were together' (Dz 3002).

> In his providence God guards and governs everything that he established, 'reaching from end to end mightily and ordering all things sweetly' (Wis 8.1). For 'all things are laid bare and are open to his eyes' (Heb 4.13) – even the things which are still to come about through the free action of creatures (Dz 3003).

To these compact paragraphs must be added the five canons of the Council which expressly condemn as heretical those views on creation which are opposed to the above teaching:

14

1. If there is anyone who denies the one, true God, Creator and Lord of visible and of invisible things – let him be anathema (Dz 3021).
2. If there is anyone who does not repent of saying that nothing exists except matter – let him be anathema (Dz 3022).
3. If there is anyone who says that the substance or essence of God and of all things is one and the same – let him be anathema (Dz 3023).
4. If there is anyone who says that both bodily and spiritual things – or spiritual things, at least – emanated from the divine substance: or that the divine essence, by a manifestation or an evolving of itself, becomes all things:

   or, finally, that God is a universal or undefined being which, by a process of self-determination, constitutes the totality of things set out into genera, species and individuals – let him be anathema (Dz 3024).
5. If there is anyone who does not confess that the world and all the things that are contained in it – both spiritual and material – have been produced in their entire substance by God out of nothing: or who says that God's will to create was not free from every kind of compulsion, but that he created as necessarily as he necessarily loves himself:

   or who denies that the world has been established for the glory of God – let him be anathema (Dz 3025).

There are certain matters in this official statement of the Church's doctrine of creation which may, for present purposes, be ignored: problems, for example, concerning divine providence, and the various heretical errors against which parts of the statement are directed. The rest provides a careful summary of traditional teaching. Indeed, the statement goes out of its way to quote (Dz 3002) a definition of the Fourth Lateran Council (A.D. 1215: cf. Dz 800); and it takes up the sense of a decree of the Council of Florence (A.D. 1442: cf. Dz 1333). Not surprisingly, therefore, it is this doctrine that is given fuller explication in every seminary textbook for the course 'On God the Creator'. At the beginning of this course a careful attempt is made to express the meaning of the official teaching.

The meaning of Vatican I's teaching

This attempt is often made by reducing the teaching to three basic *theses* or statements of position. The three theses are enunciated in some such way as the following:
1. The whole world depends in its existence totally on the activity of God the Creator.
2. God is entirely free in creating the world.
3. The ultimate purpose of the created world is to share in the goodness of God – in other words, to give glory to God.

Taken one by one, the theses can then be expounded along the following lines:

1. *The whole world depends in its existence totally on the activity of God the Creator.*

a. *The whole world...* It is clearly asserted that there is nothing 'outside' God which does not come under his creative power and activity. The notion that there could some principle or source of existence other than God is excluded. There can be no question of *dualism* – the religious or philosophical theory which would posit a source of evil alongside God who is the source of good. Absolutely everything that exists outside of God himself exists by virtue of God's creative activity.

b. *...depends in its existence...* The created world of itself – in fact, by definition – is radically non-self-sufficient with regard to its own existence. Creaturely existence derives from and continually depends on the creative power of God. It is basically contingent or dependent.

c. *...totally...* There is no part of the reality of a creature which is independent of the Creator. The entire reality, in its totality, is created and remains created. God creates the whole creature. Without creation, there is absolutely nothing of anything existing. God does not create with or out of any sort of pre-existing material. As *Creator*, precisely, he creates *out of nothing*. Where there is nothing, he creates being.

d. *...on the activity of God the Creator.* God is the full author of the whole of created reality by his creative activity. There is no question of any sort of *pantheism* – the view in which God himself is the root reality of all things. There is no question of the emanation of reality from the fulness of God's own being. God does not generate his creation out of his own nature or substance. Nor does creation come about by any kind of chance. God deliberately endows the creature with its creaturely reality by a truly creative activity which is proper to him alone as Creator. He remains radically distinct from his creation – which depends totally on him for its existence.

He is, in a true sense, the efficient or productive cause of his creation. Creation belongs to him who creates it.

2. *God is entirely free in creating the world.*

a. The act of creation is a completely free act of God's will. In creating God is free from any kind of inner or outer compulsion or necessity. He is not compelled to create by his own goodness or his own wisdom. There is no physical or moral compulsion at work in the Creator. He is free to create or not to create. He is equally free to create one kind of world or another.

b. It follows from this that the world has no necessary existence. It is radically dependent on God's free will to create. Before and until God wills to create – to use temporal terms even though God, in his eternity, is not subject to temporal duration of any kind – the world does not exist. It must thus be finite in its temporal duration. It had a beginning.

3. *The ultimate purpose of the created world is to share in the goodness of God – in other words, to give glory to God.*

a. *The ultimate purpose of the created world...* This purpose is the reason or end for which the whole creation is created by its Creator. Creation cannot have an ultimate purpose which is different from the purpose God has in creating it, since everything in creation, including its finality or purposefulness, depends totally on the Creator.

b. *...is to share in the goodness of God...* God cannot create in order to profit in any self-seeking way from his creation. He is infinitely perfect and cannot gain perfection or grow more perfect than he eternally and necessarily is. He creates in order to communicate his goodness beyond himself. He freely shares his goodness outside himself.

Not goodness merely in the sense of moral perfection or holiness, but the very goodness of his own being, the truth and reality of his own divine nature. Out of this goodness God creates in order to share it with created reality in accordance with its variable possibilities. Certain creatures will be able to share more than others, in more conscious and loving ways than others, in the divine goodness. But all creatures exist in order to share in God's goodness. He created them in a communication of his own goodness and they exist in order that they might come to share in that goodness.

c. *...in other words, to give glory to God.* 'In other words', because giving glory to God consists essentially in sharing and thereby also manifesting his goodness, as one of his creatures and part of his whole creation. In sharing the goodness of being which God communicates to his creation in creating it, the creature manifests, in the way given to it to manifest, the perfection of the Creator and his essential goodness. The creature, in other words, glorifies God; it renders, consciously or unconsciously, glory to him as Creator. And the greater the extent to which the creature shares in the God-given goodness which is its creaturely existence, the more the creature exists to the greater glory of God: the more, then, does the creature correspond to the ultimate purpose of God's whole creation.

The heavens are telling the glory of God;
and the firmament proclaims his handiwork (Ps 19.1).

Some criticisms

Such then are the three basic theses of the traditional

Church doctrine on creation very briefly and schematically expounded. There can be no denying that both the statements of the First Vatican Council quoted above and the basic theses which owe so much to them embody truths of great and permanent value and nobility. They both represent an attempt to be clear about God's creative activity, its freedom and its motive, in face of counter-attempts to dilute or confuse the truth about creation. Indeed, it is not difficult to sense throughout the Vatican statements and even the dependent theological theses the extent to which they are designed primarily to safeguard certain truths from the inroads of error. In being thus defensively intended, the statements and the theses perform, of course, a vital function in the process of handing on the Church's doctrine concerning creation. But at least one disadvantage is incurred. What is said is limited and conditioned too much by the error it seeks to refute; and so positive content and enriching enlightenment suffer in the cause of the defence of the faith. In defensive statements and theses it is not possible – and hardly opportune – to bring out the doctrine defended in all its dimensions and the full sweep of its grandeur. It is largely true that without the need to combat heresy the Church's doctrines would have hardly developed at all. Heresy has normally provided the spur for the clarification and establishment of orthodoxy. But unorthodoxy, and the consequent need for the Church's magisterium to apply correctives, can and does inhibit balanced growth in doctrine; at least in the sense that the Church is forced to reiterate and reinterpret one side of the truth – the side opposed to the error in question. The Church's reflection on her teaching has thus to be made from one angle or point of view; and so it becomes difficult for her to hold her teaching within the framework of the whole of the revelation with which she has been entrusted. The Church's teaching on creation has suffered from this kind of necessary limitation.

Again, a very dry and philosophic tone pervades the statements and the theses on creation displayed above. It is almost as if the truth that they embody were a natural truth which is attainable by the sole use of the human reason. The impression is given that a religious faith and understanding are scarcely needed for a proper grasp of the truth involved. Little stress is laid on the extent to which God reveals himself as Creator. The essentially mysterious nature of God's creative activity is largely by-passed. The rational approach to God's creation has in fact long been in fashion in the Church. It will be enough to quote the famous 'First Principle and Foundation' from the *Spiritual Exercises* of Ignatius Loyola to illustrate this statement:

> Man was created to praise, reverence and serve God our Lord, and by this means to save his soul; and the other things on the face of the earth were created for man's sake, and in order to aid him in the prosecution of the end for which he was created. Whence it follows, that man must make use of them in so far as they help him to attain his end, and in the same way he ought to withdraw himself from them in so far as they hinder him from it. It is therefore necessary that we should make ourselves indifferent to all created things, in so far as it is left to the liberty of our free will to do so, and is not forbidden; in such sort that we do not for our part wish for health

rather than sickness, for wealth rather than poverty, for honour rather than dishonour, for a long life rather than a short one; and so in all other things, desiring and choosing only those which most lead us to the end for which we were created (*Translation by John Morris, S.J.*).

If it were not clear from other sources that Ignatius was a lavishly gifted Christian mystic, it could be supposed from the view of creation apparently behind the above paragraph that he was no more than a rationalizing and calculating deist. But it has often been the case that in the Church's piety – as in her official teaching – creation has been treated as a truth entirely open to the reasonings of the human mind. The motive for such treatment has often been ascetical – to accustom Christians rightly to assess the relative value of created things and their God-given attractiveness and thus to be able to resist their charms in the struggle to achieve a total personal commitment to God when faced with his absolute claims. As a spiritual exercise this treatment of creation has considerable force. But, like the Church's official teaching, it will hardly serve to bring out the whole truth of the mystery. There is more to the truth of creation than meets the Church's official or ascetical eye.

Further, – and this is perhaps the most notable shortcoming in the Church's traditional teaching on creation – there is nothing in the official doctrine which links creation with the *Christian* revelation. In other words, creation is not presented as a specifically Christian mystery, but rather as if it were a truth which Christians held in common with non-Christians – apart, perhaps, for some minor adjustments. Creation, in the traditional presentation, has nothing to do with Christ. Yet Christ is the fulness of God's revelation. Christ represents – in fact, personally and actually *is* – God's revealing Word to men. Whatever God is believed to have revealed about himself and his saving plan in man's regard is ultimately revealed in his Christ. Creation is a revealed truth, in spite of the tendency of Church documents and presentation to make it seem not so. So creation, too, must have its place in the revelation of God which is Christ our Lord. There must be root links between Christ and creation. Yet in present-day teaching in the Church these links do not appear.

This diagnosis of what seems faulty in the Church's traditional teaching on creation is not to be read as a disloyal protest against the teaching authority of the Church. It represents, on the contrary, a complaint that the Church's official teaching has not yet gone far enough in the elucidation of the revealed truth of creation. There are sound historical reasons why the Church should have limited herself to emphasizing certain aspects of the truth. Other, and deeper, aspects still remain to be investigated. And it is the task of the Church's theologians to pursue the investigation into the fuller mystery of creation where the Church's official teaching stops short. In particular, it is the theologian's task to bring the full light of God's revelation in Christ to bear on creation. But how does the theologian go about remedying what he finds inadequate in the Church's doctrine? On what lines must the necessary readjustment proceed?

A new procedure

It seems clear that the doctrine of creation needs a treatment which will proceed along two – though not radically distinct – lines. In the first place, the doctrine must be brought within the general Christian mystery of salvation. One of the chief inadequacies in the presentation of the doctrine has been that creation has seemed to stand outside the salvific work of God in man's regard. Salvation has been seen solely as God's reaction to sin. Creation preceded salvation and has no intrinsic connection with it. Creation could be looked on as an activity of God which belongs to the distant past. The believer had to be more interested in salvation, which concerns his personal present and future in a way that creation could not. But this distinction between creation and salvation – often thought to be the grounds of the so-called natural and supernatural orders respectively – is not tenable in the full light of God's revelation in Christ. Creation must be seen as a first but essential step in the unfolding of the history of salvation.

In the second place, the doctrine of creation needs to be brought into real and direct connection with the incarnate centre of the mystery of salvation, Christ our Lord. It is idle to disregard or to neglect the scriptural evidence for the link between Christ and God's creation. To locate creation as a divine activity which is 'already' Christoform is a demand both of sound scriptural scholarship and sane Christian theology.

What follows is an attempt to pursue the elucidation of the Christian mystery of creation along the lines indicated. This foray into ways of considering creation which are widely unfamiliar draws strength from the Church's doctrine, and seeks only to build upon it.

CHAPTER 2

BIBLICAL FAITH IN GOD THE CREATOR

It is of first importance to examine the Old Testament writings in order to see how Israel came to believe in creation. It would be quite wrong to suppose that Israel's faith in God was, from the beginning, faith in God the Creator. While it is true that the Bible begins with two different 'accounts' of the creation, both of these passages are of relatively late composition. The second of them (Gen 2.4b-25) is the earlier of the two, and may have been written in the ninth or eighth century B.C. It belongs to a tradition of writing called the 'Yahwistic' tradition, since the name of God it uses is the name which God revealed to Moses – Yahweh. The first account of creation (Gen 1.1-2.4a) is of considerably later date, possibly as late as the fifth century B.C. This account comes from another tradition of writing altogether, the 'Priestly' tradition, in which interest centres on the law and on the liturgy of Israel. The inclusion of these two accounts of creation in their present position at the beginning of the book of Genesis does not mean that the faith of Israel first began with God the Creator. This is not to say, of course, that Israel did not believe at all in God the Creator before such a late stage in her religious history. But the full formulation and expression of that faith developed out of her faith in another aspect of God's activity with regard to his chosen people.

Israel's faith in God was first and foremost faith in God the Saviour – God who personally, that is, freely and lovingly, intervened in human history in favour of his chosen people. An early kind of 'creed' declared this faith in God:

A wandering Aramean was my father; and he went down into Egypt and sojourned there, few in number; and there he became a nation, great, mighty, and populous. And the Egyptians treated us harshly, and afflicted us, and laid upon us hard bondage. Then we cried to the Lord the God of our fathers, and the Lord heard our voice, and saw our affliction, our toil, and our oppression; and the Lord brought us out of Egypt with a mighty hand and an outstretched arm, with great terror, with signs and wonders; and he brought us into this place and gave us this land, a land flowing with milk and honey (Deut 26.5-9).

It was not in the wonders or in the order of nature that Israel first came to know God, but in his saving actions in history on Israel's behalf. It was because God could exercise such obvious mastery over the events and course of history as he displayed in his saving actions for Israel that in time Israel came to see that he exercised a similar – but wider – mastery over the whole of nature. Israel's God made use of the elements – sun, rain, dew, thunder, lightning, wind and so on – to bring about his purposeful plan in history. He could give riches, multiply flocks, divide the Red Sea waters, rain down manna on his people in the desert and give them water from a rock to drink.

Israel's faith in God was primarily a belief that he who did all these things for them was their God. Their God showed, through his saving activity on behalf of his people, that he was master of the universe and its forces. Slowly the way was being prepared for the explicit belief that the God who was master of the forces of nature and the events of history was also the creator of the whole universe in which those forces and events were at play.

By a late seventh century prophet like Jeremiah creation is still considered not so much as God's bringing all things into existence as an act of God the Saviour, who takes part in Israel's history:

> It is I who by my great power and my outstretched arm have made the earth, with the men and animals that are on the earth, and I give it to whomever it seems right to me. Now I have given all these lands into the hands of Nebuchadnezzar, the king of Babylon, my servant, and I have given him also the beasts of the field to serve his (Jer 27.5f.).

Again, Jeremiah's God mentions his creative activity to strengthen his claim over his people:

> Do you not fear me? says the Lord; Do you not tremble before me? I placed the sand as the bound for the sea, a perpetual barrier which it cannot pass; though the waves toss, they cannot prevail, though they roar they cannot pass over it. But this people has a stubborn and rebellious heart; they have turned aside and gone away (Jer 5.22f.).

The vast and ordered work of God's creation is the true measure of God's devotion to his people:

> Thus says the Lord,
> who gives the sun for light by day

and the fixed order of the moon
and the stars for light by night,
who stirs up the sea so that its waves roar –
the Lord of hosts is his name:
'If this fixed order departs
from before me,' says the Lord,
'then shall the descendants of Israel cease
from being a nation before me for ever.'
Thus says the Lord:
'If the heavens above can be measured,
and the foundations of the earth below can be
    explored,
then I will cast off all the descendants of Israel
for all that they have done, says the Lord.' (Jer 31.35-37)

For Jeremiah creation is the mighty act of a God who will remain faithful to his people. Creation is not considered outside the context of God's relationship to Israel.

Faith in God the Creator

A decisive breakthrough in the understanding and expression of Israel's faith in God as Creator came in the writings of the unknown sixth-century prophet called Second or Deutero-Isaiah, whose work forms the second part of the book of Isaiah (chapters 40-55). From the first verses of these chapters (Is 40.1f.) this part of Isaiah has been called 'The Book of the Consolation of Israel'. It was written during the difficult days of Israel's exile in Babylonia in order to comfort and encourage God's people, surrounded as they were by the cults of alien deities and longing to return to their homeland and to the worship of their God. It is hardly surprising that Israel, under the pressure of the exile, should seek out and find new and deeper truths about its God. They were forced to ask what their God's overall position was. On what overriding truth about its God could Israel base its hopes in such a hopeless situation? It was under the impact of the exile situation that Israel began to see clearly that the God who in the past had saved Israel from the Egyptian captivity, and who, they must hope, would save Israel from the Babylonian exile, had a universal 'saving' function with regard to the whole universe. In this Israel's God immeasurably surpassed the weird divinities of Babylon. He it was who originally 'saved' the universe out of chaos: in other words, who *created* the universe by an act of masterful, victorious power. This creative act of Israel's God must have been the first of all his interventions in history. In fact, Israel's God *began* all history with his *fiat*; and it is his saving purpose which alone gives sense and meaning to history. Amid the hardships of the exile Israel sought for the meaning of its troubled history, and found it in the God who created all things, and who controlled all events, and who thus must also have the power to fulfil once again his loving purpose towards his chosen people.

The amazingly rich thought of Second Isaiah can only be appreciated in a continuous reading of his brilliant prophecies. The abundance of themes which bear on the author's faith in God the Creator has to be savoured as it stands. The consolation of the exiled Israel lies in the utter faithfulness of Israel's God, who first selected and formed Israel to be his servant. Israel's God cannot forget his people. He will forgive their shortcomings, redeem them from their sins. The past events of Israel's history

will be re-enacted for their benefit. There will be a new
Exodus, like the great Exodus from Egypt. There will be
a new covenant of peace, as in the days of Noah; a new
start for the people, as in the days of Abraham; a renewal
of God's relationship of love for David. There will even
be a new creation in favour of Israel. Present distress will
pass, for Israel's God is above all nations, above their
rulers and above their gods. Israel's God is no hand-made
idol. Even King Cyrus, Israel's overlord, is no more than
a tool of God's purposes. Israel's God is unsurpassable
in wisdom, in strength. He is incomparable. He will give
victory to Israel, and through Israel reveal his salvation
to the ends of the earth.

The most strikingly new element which emerged in
Second Isaiah's faith in God was one which could only
emerge in Israel's encounter with foreign gods: there was
in fact no God other than Israel's own God. Israel's God
alone exists and has the power to act:

> Before me no god was formed,
> nor shall there be any after me.
> I, I am the Lord,
> and besides me there is no saviour.
> I declared and saved and proclaimed,
> when there was no strange god among you;
> and you are my witnesses, says the Lord.
> I am God, and also henceforth I am He;
> there is none who can deliver from my hand;
> I work and who can hinder it? (Is 43.10-13).

The God of Israel openly declares himself to be the one
and only God, from the beginning to the end (Is 41.4;
44.6; 48.12). His purpose alone will prevail:

> For I am God, and there is no other;

> I am God, and there is none like me,
> declaring the end from the beginning
> and from ancient times things not yet done,
> saying, 'My counsel shall stand,
> and I will accomplish all my purpose',
> calling a bird of prey from the east,
> the man of my counsel from a far country.
> I have spoken, and I will bring it to pass;
> I have purposed, and I will do it (Is 46.9-11).

It is out of the background of this complete monotheism, in which Israel is promised certain release from the Babylonian captivity at the hands of her one and only true God, that a fully developed faith in God the Creator emerges.

> Hearken to me, O Jacob,
> and Israel, whom I called!
> I am He, I am the first,
> and I am the last.
> My hand laid the foundation of the earth,
> and my right hand spread out the heavens;
> when I call to them,
> they stand forth together (Is 48.12f.).

There can have been no greater consolation for exiled Israel than to hear that the God who had made Israel his own had also made all things his own from the beginning, when he created them:

> Thus says the Lord, your Redeemer,
> who formed you from the womb:
> 'I am the Lord who made all things,
> who stretched out the heavens alone,
> who spread out the earth – Who was with me?'
>   (Is 44.24).

31

Israel's God was he of whom it could be said: 'The Lord is the everlasting God, the Creator of the ends of the earth' (Is 40.28). He created heaven and earth and gave life to every human being (cf. Is 42.5). He was man's Maker (cf. Is 45.9-12), who had not created earth a chaos, but made it an inhabitable world for men (cf. Is 45.18).

This Creator God is pictured in his creative activity: measuring the waters, marking off the heavens, gathering the earth and weighing the mountains and hills (cf. Is 40.12). He sits above the earth, its inhabitants like grass-hoppers beneath him, stretching and spreading out the heavens like a curtain or a tent (cf. Is 40.22). He calls into existence every single star of all the millions that exist (cf. Is 40.26). Israel's faith in God the Saviour of his people was thus enriched by the inspired insight of Second Isaiah: the Saviour God would and could surely save Israel once again. There could be no opposition to him in the long run. He is the one and only God, respon-sible alike for the furtherance of his purposes on earth, the heavens, the universe and all things and all men in it. From faith in God the Saviour developed a wider and deeper faith in God the Creator of all things. Israel cannot be left widowed by God:

> For your Maker is your husband,
> the Lord of hosts is his name;
> And the Holy One of Israel is your Redeemer,
> the God of the whole earth he is called (Is 54.5).

Genesis and Creation

In the wake of this outstanding development in Israel's faith came the opportunity for an expression of faith in

God the Creator outside the explicit context of faith in God the Saviour. This is the case with the two accounts of Creation already mentioned above – which stand at the beginning of the book of Genesis. To have considered them in detail at the start of this chapter would have masked that development in Israel's faith which alone provides a correct background for the undistorted understanding of them. The placing of the two accounts – one of them already of considerable antiquity – in their present position was Israel's way of expressing her new-found faith in God the Creator. They are *not*, of course, Israel's way of answering a scientific question about the origins of the universe. Israel was given to declaring the overall mastery of the God who was her Saviour, not to cosmological curiosity. The two accounts, of unequal age and disparate background and somewhat clumsily set side by side, express in the eyes of Israel's faith what must have been the first intervention of Israel's Saviour God in the affairs of his world – its creation.

The second account (Gen 2.4b-25), as has been said, is the earlier by perhaps three centuries. The main interest lies not in creation as such but in the formation and special position of man in a world which God made for him to inhabit and rule. God, who is evidently supreme and sole maker of all that exists, works against a rural background. He works like a human potter when he forms man from the dust of the ground; and like a human farmer when he plants his garden in Eden. Man is God's creature in a special sense. Unlike the plants and birds and beasts, man lives with a life directly derived from the life of God himself (Gen 2.7). Man has intelligence: the power to name all the other creatures and the power to obey God.

And man is a social being, deriving help from, and giving love to, his female counterpart. This primitive account of creation and man's special place in God's scheme of things served to express Israel's faith in a God whose original intention it must have been that every man should acknowledge and obey him. Man was created and put on earth by God to work for God his maker.

The first account of creation (Gen 1.1-2.4a) is much more complex and sophisticated. In the first place, it is important to realize the highly formalized structure given to God's creative activity in this account. Eight 'works' of creation are spread over six 'days' of creation. The first four 'works', in the first three 'days', form a group in which God separates the main parts of the universe from one another. The second four 'works', in the second three 'days', form another group in which God furnishes the universe he has prepared. Thus:

Day 1   Light and darkness separated as day and
        night
    2   Upper and lower waters separated by
        heaven
    3 (a) Earth and seas separated
      (b) Vegetation grows on earth
    4   Lights of the heavens made (sun, moon,
        stars)
    5   Fishes and birds made
    6 (a) Animals of the earth made
      (b) Man made.

This artificial structure has been imposed on God's creative activity in the interests of the 'Priestly' tradition from which this account comes. The six 'days' of God's activity followed by a seventh 'day' of divine rest are

34

held out as the model for the working week of the pious Jew for whom the observation of the Sabbath's rest from profane activity is a key element of religion. Again, the grandiose orderliness of the account, with its works of separation and of furnishing, and with its geocentric pattern in which man stands at the summit of God's achievement, brings out the special place which man is believed to have in God's designs. He is created last and is given dominion over the rest of the living creation. What is more important, he alone is created with an inborn affinity to God himself: 'Let us make man in our image, after our likeness... So God created man in his own image, in the image of God he created him' (Gen 1.26f.). Beneath the formalized structure of this account of creation can be discerned the deep conviction about the status and value of man which flowed from Israel's faith in God the Creator.

But, in the second place, it is Israel's convictions about God the Creator himself that clearly emerge from this account. In order to appreciate the scope and importance of these convictions it is necessary to consider the sort of creation-account that was current among Israel's neighbours at the time when Israel produced this one. In the lands of Mesopotamia and in Canaan itself there were a number of highly mythological accounts of creation. The best known is that found in the Mesopotamian epic called *Enuma Elish*. In the beginning there is chaos – a hostile and formless monster, identified with the primordial ocean which attacks the land ceaselessly. This chaos is identified with two gods, a male god called Apsû and – importantly for present purposes – a goddess called Tiāmat. They produce other gods. Apsû is killed, leaving Tiāmat as the monster of chaos who spawns a horde of demons to help her in the fight against her original offspring led by Marduk. Marduk, however, kills Tiämat, and from the dead material creates the visible universe – the earth like a disk resting on the abyss of the sea. There is an overarching sky in which the stars move; and over the sky are the chambers of the wind and the rain. The gods live in the heavenly bodies, and Marduk himself lives in a heavenly palace. Man is made of clay mixed with the blood of a god who was an ally of Tiämat and was killed. Man was created to carry on the cult of the gods. In this account creation is out of pre-existing, divine, chaotic material, following on the victory of Marduk over Tiämat. But the victory was not final. Creative power must constantly reassert itself over the power of chaos.

Whilst there are undoubtedly elements in this quaint and fearsome myth which make their mark in the first Genesis account of creation, there are many points of vital difference which show how purer and more advanced Israel's faith in God the Creator was than the superstitions of her neighbours. Israel's faith is completely monotheistic. There is one God alone who totally transcends all created reality and has uncontested dominion over it. There is no question of a time when he did not exist: he is pre-existent, equivalently eternal. His creative action is spontaneous and unassisted by anything outside himself. That action is described by a Hebrew word (*bārā'* = 'created') which is reserved in the Bible – and is especially popular with Second Isaiah – for the distinctively mighty and wondrous acts of God. God acts simply through his word, by the sheer expression of his will: 'And God said... And it was so'. And his creative action covers the whole of reality as it appeared to the unscientific eyes of the author of the account. There is nothing outside of God which God did not create. Most tellingly, God's creative activity is not a combat with a hostile monster. There is no primitive chaos opposed to God's purposes. The Hebrew word *tehôm*, which is linked with the Tiāmat of the myth, has no divine properties. Chaos is reduced to the shapeless and unresisting matter in which God creates what he wants, as he wants. It would be difficult to maintain that the first Genesis account expressly teaches that God created all things out of nothing. The notion of 'nothing' was unimaginable to the unphilosophical author, but he can still get across the essential truth that whatever does exist was created by God. For this reason everything that exists is good, as the author repeatedly insists. There is no dualism of a good and a bad principle at play in the work of creation. Evil did not exist alongside God, and cannot have come from him. Man, too, stands in a privileged position, directly and specially created by God with God-like qualities: no mixture of clay and a dead god's blood.

In fact it is obvious that the first Genesis account does more than build on the ideas in neighbouring myths. It systematically contradicts those mythical notions which could not possibly be consonant with Israel's faith in the Saviour God who is also acknowledged to be the Creator of all things. While it is true that the basic world-picture of the Genesis account is the same as that of the myth described above – the author did not have the scientific knowledge which alone would have helped him to go against the appearances of the heavens and the earth – there lurks in the account more than a hint of directly polemical purpose. Israel was asserting faith in the

Creator God in face of surrounding error. Thus, for instance, not only is Tiāmat/*tehôm* fully 'de-mythologized', but the heavenly bodies, which were the homes of the gods in the Mesopotamian myth, are no more than God-given ways of telling the time in the Genesis account. The account is wrongly understood if it is thought to have any scientific aim. It is a highly elaborate expression of Israel's faith in a God who has continually saved her, and who will save her in the future, in virtue of his original and easy mastery over everything that exists – as Creator. It is an expression of faith made in opposition to current trends of thought, yet dependent on the contemporary world-picture.

It is interesting to see how Israel's faith in God the Creator could, without any real danger of misunderstanding, go on expressing itself in terms of the old creation myths. Even Second Isaiah can appeal to God's ancient victory over Rahab, a sea-dragon not unlike Tiāmat:

> Awake, awake, put on strength,
> O arm of the Lord;
> awake as in the days of old,
> the generations of long ago.
> Was it not thou that didst cut Rahab in pieces,
> that didst pierce the dragon? (Is 51.9; cf. Job 9.13;
> Ps 89.10).

Sometimes creation is likened to the slaying of Leviathan, a many-headed sea-serpent (e.g. Is 27.1; Ps 74.14). But the use of the old mythical figures is no more than a poetical attempt to express, in the most picturesque language available, the might of God's creative action. In fact, the old figures are quite neutralised in these lively expressions of Israel's faith. The horrid monsters of the past are reduced to creatures of God like all the rest:

> Yonder is the sea, great and wide,
> which teems with things innumerable,
> living things both small and great.
> There go the ships,
> and Leviathan which thou didst form to sport in it
> (Ps 104.25f.).

Similarly, it is hardly to be expected that the world-picture in Israel's expressions of faith would be different from that of contemporary creation myths. Quite apart from the fact that it was not the intention of the author of the first Genesis account to correct the picture of the physical world as he and the mythmakers knew it, there was no scientific means whereby such an adjustment could have been made. Hence the structure and furniture of the universe in the Old Testament remain such as they would have been seen through pre-scientific eyes (cf. e.g., Job 38.4-38; Ps 33.6f.; Ps 104.2-9; Prov 8.26-29).

The sense of creation

But in spite of what seem to the modern reader to be childish crudities and all-too-human limitations there is no doubt that along with faith in God the Creator went a very lively sense of the createdness of things. This is evident in an early prophet like Amos (4.13; 5.8), and most emphatically in Psalm 104. Here all the abundance of nature – waters, vegetation, vines, crops, birds, beasts – is attributed to the creative action of God. Indeed, there is a real sense in which Israel considered creation not only as a past and mighty deed of God, but also as a present activity of God. The natural alternation of light and darkness, day and night, was known, of course, to depend on the presence or absence of the sun. But behind it lay the still creating hand of God, making darkness (Ps 104.19f.), calling out the stars to their nightly existence (Is 40.26), still calling the world into existence:

> My hand laid the foundation of the earth,
> and my right hand spread out the heavens;
> When I call to them,
> they stand forth together (Is 48.13).

The existence of things is a matter of constantly renewed life which derives from God:

> When thou hidest thy face, they are dismayed;
> when thou takest away their breath, they die
> and return to their dust.
> When thou sendest forth thy Spirit [or 'breath'] they
> are created;
> and thou renewest the face of the ground (Ps 104.29f.).

The most intimate sense of createdness is that which man has concerning himself. God 'gives breath to the people upon' the earth, 'and spirit to those who walk in it' (Is 42.5). Job acknowledges how God fashioned him in every detail (Job 10.8-12), and both Jeremiah (18.1-6) and Isaiah (64.8) liken God to a potter who is completely responsible for the shape and purpose of his product, man. The whole of Psalm 139 is the cry of one who realizes his inescapable and total dependence on God his Creator. Along with the sense of createdness goes the conviction of God-given dignity of man and lordship over the rest of creation: 'thou hast made him little less than God, and dost crown him with glory and honour' (cf. Ps 8.3-8).

40

Man is in a position to see that the whole of creation is God's, by virtue of his creation of it, and that it thus leads man to praise and glorify him who created it (cf. e.g. Ps 19.1-6; 24.1f.; 89.5-12; 95.1-7).

The depth and strength of Old Testament faith in God the Creator is nowhere better attested than in the encouragement given by a mother to the seventh son of hers she saw martyred in one day in the persecution of the Jews by Antiochus in the second century B.C.:

> I do not know how you came into being in my womb. It was not I who gave you life and breath, nor I who set in order the elements within each of you. Therefore the Creator of the world, who shaped the beginning of man and devised the origin of all things, will in his mercy give life and breath back to you again... I beseech you, my child, to look at the heaven and the earth and see everything that is in them, and recognize that God did not make them out of things that existed. Thus also mankind comes into being... (2 Macc 7.22f., 28).

Not only does this mother's speech display the sustaining power that faith in God the Creator had come to have among the Jews; it also shows how, through contact with Greek thinking, the Jews were able to make clear, in a way that had been beyond the author of the first Genesis account, that God created what exists out of nothing. The myth of pre-existing chaos, independent of God, had been finally laid to rest.

It was this firm and lively Old Testament faith in God the Creator, developed in the course of time out of Israel's basic faith in God the Saviour, that the New Testament

41

presupposes. There was little room for the further development of Israel's faith, so deeply had it taken root by New Testament times in the religious consciousness of the Jews. Naturally faith in God the Creator was already part of the beliefs of those who first witnessed in writing to the truth of Christ. So it is simply taken for granted that creation had a beginning (Mk 10.6; 13.19; Mt 19.4); and that the world underwent a 'foundation' at God's hands (Mt 13.35; 25.34; Lk 11.50; Jn 17.24; Eph 1.4; Heb 4.3; 9.26; 1 Pet 1.20; Apoc 13.8; 17.8). In the preaching of the early Church there was nothing excepted from God's creation (Acts 4.24; 14.15; 17.24; cf. 1 Cor 10.26; 1 Tim 6.13; Apoc 10.6). God 'calls into existence the things that do not exist' (Rom 4.17).

The fact that God created everything sets up an enduring relationship between him and created things: 'in him we live and move and have our being', as St Paul quotes from an ancient poet (Acts 17.28). The createdness of things is such as to condemn those who refuse to acknowledge it:

> For what can be known about God is plain to them,
> because God has shown it to them. Ever since the
> creation of the world his invisible nature, namely
> his eternal power and deity, has been clearly per-
> ceived in the things that have been made. So they
> are without excuse (Rom 1.19f.).

That same createdness evokes praise of the Creator: 'For from him and through him and to him are all things. To him be glory for ever' (Rom 11.36). Or as St John puts it:

> Worthy art thou, our Lord and God,
> to receive glory and honour and power,

for thou didst create all things,
and by thy will they existed and were created.
    (Apoc 4.11).

The biblical faith in God the Creator was thus largely a product of the experience of Old Testament writers who, under the inspiration of God himself, were able to expand Israel's faith in her *salvation* at the hands of God to the *creation* of all things at the hands of one and the same God. God the Creator came to be experienced in faith with the same continuous clarity as God the Saviour made his presence and his power felt in and through his interventions in history on Israel's behalf. Indeed creation is only the first act in the historical drama of salvation. As that drama further unfolded itself in the coming of Christ, faith in God the Creator did not need to change. But it came to be clarified and intensified in a way that must be examined further.

CHAPTER 3

THE BIBLICAL THEOLOGY OF GOD'S CREATION

The origin and extent of the biblical faith in God the Creator has been briefly outlined in the preceding chapter. It is now time to consider further how and in what terms the biblical writers understood their faith in creation. How did they imagine or conceptualize the mystery of creation in which they believed? To answer this question is to begin to expound their *theology* of creation – how they sought to render creation intelligible to themselves and thus transmissible to others. Obviously what is possible for biblical writers will seem to fall far short of what will be possible later for Christian theologians and philosophers who have much more refined conceptual tools to work with in their reflections on the mystery of creation. But what the biblical theologian will lack in refinement and exactitude, he will often gain in directness and force. What is more, it is part of the Christian faith to believe that the biblical theologian is inspired in his task in a special way not shared by the more sophisticated thinkers of a later age. So it will be well worthwhile to try and see how the biblical theology of God's creation developed.

Word and Wisdom in the Old Testament

Israel's faith in God the Creator, as has been seen, developed out of faith in God the Saviour in face of the hardships of exile and the challenge of alien gods. It came to

contain the key conviction that God created all things –
out of nothing, as the later Jews came to hold – by the
sheer expression of his sovereign will: in a word, by his
Word. This conviction plays a large part in the first
Genesis account of creation: 'And God said... And it
was so'. It seems that, for the Jew, the speaking of a word,
accompanied necessarily by the release of the breath,
denoted the exercise of inward power on outward reality.
At any rate, this thought seems to be behind the following:

> Let all thy creatures serve thee,
>
> for thou didst speak, and they were made.
>
> Thou didst send forth thy Spirit [or 'breath'],
>
> and it formed them;
>
> there is none that can resist thy voice (Judith 16.14).

The thought is expanded in the Psalms:

> By the word of the Lord the heavens were made,
>
> and all their host by the breath of his mouth...
>
> For he spoke, and it, the earth, came to be;
>
> he commanded and it stood forth (Ps 33.6,9).

God's word is the prompt executor of his will in creation:

> He sends forth his command to the earth;
>
> his word runs swiftly (Ps 147.15).

But in time Israel's faith came to accept a somewhat more
elaborate conviction – that God created by an exercise
of his Wisdom. Wisdom, for the Jew, was not so much an
intellectual virtue as a practical knowledge of how to do
things, a *savoir faire*, much prized generally in the Near
East. If one thing was evident to the man who contem-
plated God's work of creation it was that the Creator
possessed wisdom in a surpassing degree: not only, then,
the power of creating by a mere word, but the wisdom to
create a world of wondrous design.

O Lord, how manifold are thy works!
In wisdom hast thou made them all;
the earth is full of thy creatures (Ps 104.24).

It is in the Sapiential, or 'Wisdom', books of the Old Testament that this conviction was most clearly elaborated. God's wisdom came to be personified and presented as a divine quality or entity, not distinct from God, but not totally identified with him either. And as the elaboration of the figure of Wisdom proceeded, Wisdom took on the status, it might almost be said, of a second divine person.

When God spoke to Job out of the whirlwind it was to impress on him the extent to which God's works surpass human understanding and wisdom (Job 38-39). The wisdom of God, manifest in those works, escapes the grasp of mere man:

But where shall wisdom be found?
And where is the place of understanding?
Man does not know the way to it,
and it is not found in the land of the living...
God understands the way to it,
and knows its place.
For he looks to the ends of the earth,
and sees everything under the heavens.
When he gave to the wind its weight,
and meted out the waters by measure;
when he made a decree for the rain,
and a way for the lightning of the thunder;
then he saw it and declared it;
he established it, and searched it out (Job 28.12f., 23-27).

The creation was an exercise and product of God's wisdom. God is 'the fountain of wisdom' (Bar 3.12):

> He who knows all things knows her,
> he found her by his understanding.
> He who prepared the earth for all time
> filled it with four-footed creatures;
> he who sends forth the light and it goes,
> called it, and it obeyed him in fear... (Bar 3.31-33).

In the collection of proverbs which stands at the head of the Book of Proverbs (1.1-9.18), and which is probably of the fourth or third century B.C., the role of God's wisdom and understanding in creation (cf. 3.19f.) is vividly described by personified Wisdom herself in a passage of the greatest importance (8.22-31). In an earlier speech (1.22-33) she had already spoken in a way which asserted her divine status. But in the later speech she claims to be the very first of God's works, produced before the creation of any reality external to God (8.22-26). Further, when God performed his work of the world's creation, she was present – and not merely as a spectator:

> I was beside him, like a master workman;
> and I was daily his delight,
> rejoicing in his inhabited world
> and delighting in the sons of men (Prov 8.30f.).

To claim a special origin, prior to creation, from God, along with an active part in the divine work of creation, is to claim to be, in a way that was at this time by no means clear, equivalently divine, as God himself is divine, and yet somehow distinct from God. Later New Testament writers will see their way to being more precise about Wisdom's status, but for the present that status remains obscurely mysterious.

It is the same in the Wisdom of Jesus the son of Sirach,

a second-century B.C. book often called 'Ecclesiasticus'. Once again, Wisdom appears as a female figure mysteriously produced, before the creation of external reality, by God himself (Ecclus 1.4-9). And once again it is in a speech that Wisdom herself reveals her origin, her status and her role in creation. She 'came forth from the mouth of the Most High' (Ecclus 24.3) – an origin which obviously makes her equivalent to God's breath or Word. She is plainly eternal:

> From eternity, in the beginning, he created me,
>
> and for eternity I shall not cease to exist (Ecclus 24.9).

She had a special function with regard to creation: she
> covered the earth like a mist...
>
> Alone I have made the circuit of the vault of heaven
>
> and have walked in the depths of the abyss (Ecclus 24.3,5).

And she claims qualities which point to her divinity (Ecclus 24.4,6,10-17).

Still more elaborated is the description of Wisdom in the first century B.C. Book of Wisdom. 'Who more than she is the fashioner of what exists'? (Wis 8.6): for
> with thee is wisdom, who knows thy works
>
> and was present when thou didst make the world...
>
> (Wis 9.9).

The author of the book thus eulogizes Wisdom and her role in creation:

> Wisdom, the fashioner of all things, taught me. For in her there is a spirit that is intelligent, holy, unique, manifold, subtle, mobile, clear, unpolluted, distinct, invulnerable, loving the good, keen, irresistible, beneficent, humane, steadfast, sure, free from anxiety, all-powerful, overseeing all, and

penetrating through all spirits that are intelligent and pure and most subtle. For wisdom is more mobile than any motion; because of her pureness she pervades and penetrates all things. For she is a breath of the power of God, and a pure emanation of the glory of the Almighty... For she is a reflection of eternal light, a spotless mirror of the working of God, and an image of his goodness... She reaches mightily from one end of the earth to the other, and she orders all things well (Wis 7.22-26; 8.1).

The Old Testament contains no more developed a description of the enigmatic figure of Wisdom than this. But the development that has been traced here was to prove invaluable to writers of the New Testament books for their expression of the personal reality of him whom they acknowledged as their Lord and Saviour. The figure of Wisdom, of divine status and with a special function with regard to God's creation as a whole, mysteriously born of God himself, and active in God's own creative activity, was seen to fit with what the first Christians came to realize, in faith, about Jesus Christ and about his relationship to all that existed.

Wisdom in the New Testament

There are indications in the gospels that Christ himself may have interpreted his person and his function in terms of the Old Testament figure of Wisdom. Whether this interpretation in terms of Wisdom featured among other interpretations given by the risen Christ to the disciples with whom he walked to Emmaus, when 'beginning with Moses and all the prophets, he interpreted to them in *all* the Scriptures the things concerning himself' (Lk 24.27), cannot, of course, be known. But when Christ, in one of his attacks on the Pharisees, told them that 'the queen of the South will arise at the judgment with this generation and condemn it; for she came from the ends of the earth to hear the wisdom of Solomon, and behold, something greater than Solomon is here' (Mt 12.42; cf. Lk 11.31), he appears to be placing himself in the context of divine Wisdom. Similarly with the well-known words of Mt 11.28-30–

> Come to me, all who labour and are heavy laden, and I will give you rest. Take my yoke upon you, and learn from me; for I am gentle and lowly in heart, and you will find rest for your souls. For my yoke is easy, and my burden is light

– it is fairly clear that Christ is speaking with the accents of Wisdom in Ecclus 24.19-22.

St Paul, whose knowledge of the Wisdom literature and its rabbinic interpretation derived from his early training, certainly interpreted Christ in terms of the figure of Wisdom. Thus, in a passage which owes everything to what he had learnt from the rabbis (1 Cor 10.1-5), he tells how the Israelites who escaped from Egypt were sheltered by a cloud, how they passed through the Red Sea, and how they were sustained in the wilderness: 'for they drank from the supernatural Rock which followed them, and the Rock was Christ' (1 Cor 10.4). In the Book of Wisdom it is the figure of Wisdom herself who shelters the Israelites, brings them through the sea, and slakes their thirst in the desert: 'when they thirsted they called upon thee, and water was given them out of the flinty rock, the slaking of thirst from hard stone... thou gavest them abundant water unexpectedly' (Wis 11.4,7; cf. 10.15-11.8). In St Paul's mind there is a significant equivalence between Christ and Wisdom. At other times St Paul can be more explicit: he calls 'Christ the power of God and the wisdom of God' (1 Cor 1.24), and his preaching of Christ crucified to the Corinthians was not the imparting of–

> a wisdom of this age or of the rulers of this age, who
> are doomed to pass away. But we impart a secret
> and hidden wisdom of God, which God decreed
> before the ages for our glorification (1 Cor 2.6f).

It is, however, not so much the direct identification of Christ with Old Testament Wisdom that is the most striking New Testament use of the figure of Wisdom; rather it is the actual ascription to Christ of the qualities, status and role of Wisdom as described in the Wisdom books quoted above. In studying this ascription – more extensive in the New Testament than is commonly realized – it can be seen how Christ came to be linked with the divine activity of creation.

In the first place, there was ascribed to Christ the quality of likeness to God. He was believed to be the image of God himself. This is the implication of a number of statements made by the Christ of St John's Gospel. The Father remains invisible to men, but he has revealed himself visibly in Christ his Son. 'No one has ever seen God; the only Son, who is in the bosom of the Father, he has made him known' (Jn 1.18). So to the queries of Thomas and Philip Christ can answer: 'If you had known me, you would have known my Father also; henceforth you know him and have seen him... He who has seen me has seen the Father...' (Jn 14.7,9; cf. 6.36). Likeness to God, being an image of God, is a quality of Wisdom: 'For she is a reflection of eternal light, a spotless mirror of the working of God, and an image of his goodness' (Wis 7.26). And the author of the Letter to the Hebrews says much the same of Christ: 'he reflects the glory of God and bears the very stamp of his nature' (Heb 1.3). St Paul, once again, is quite explicit: 'Christ... is the likeness of God' (2 Cor 4.4); 'he is the image of the invisible God' (Col 1.15). Nor does St Paul mean that Christ is an empty, purely earthly reflection of God. He means to say that in being God's image and likeness Christ is truly and fully God in person. Christ 'was in the form of God' (Phil 2.6); 'he was rich' (2 Cor 8.9) – rich in the sense that 'in him the fulness of God was pleased to dwell' (Col 1.19), 'for in him the whole fulness of deity dwells bodily' (Col 2.9). Like Old Testament Wisdom, Christ was seen to be the likeness and image of God himself.

Again, in a way that closely followed the Old Testament figure of Wisdom, Christ was considered in the New Testament to have a special status vis-à-vis God – a status that was prior to, and connected with, the creative activity of God. It is this status which is meant when it is said that Christ is 'the first-born' (Heb 1.6). Behind this title lies a long tradition of biblical thinking, according to which the first-born represents the finest production of an animal or human parent. As Jacob said of his son Reuben: 'my first-born, my might, and the first-fruits of my strength, pre-eminent in pride and pre-eminent in power' (Gen 49.3; cf. Deut 21.17; Ps 89.19-37). As in the case of the figure of Wisdom, Christ came to be considered as having existed 'from the beginning' (1 Jn 1.1; 2.13f.). Not only did the prophet Isaiah see his glory and speak of him (Jn 12.41); not only did Christ himself claim to pre-date Abraham (Jn 8.56-58); but he himself could also refer to that state of glory which he had with his Father 'before the foundation of the world' (Jn 17.24; cf. 17.5). St Paul says that 'he is before all things' (Col 1.17); and it is to this pre-existent state of Christ, the Word, that St John refers at the start of his Gospel, in words which consciously echo the opening words of the book of Genesis: 'In the beginning was the Word, and the Word was with God, and the Word was God. He was in the beginning with God' (Jn 1.1-2). The claim of Wisdom to exist with God from eternity was verified, to the faith of the New Testament theologians, in Christ.

And likewise also Wisdom's claim to have been active in creation along with God was seen to apply to Christ. He is 'the first-born of all creation' (Col 1.15); 'the beginning of God's creation' (Apoc 3.14). The sense is not that Christ himself was thought to be one creature among all the rest of God's productions, but that he is the principle or starting-point of God's creative activity. St John expresses this sense when, attributing to Christ the status with regard to creation which God claimed for himself in Isaiah (41.4; 44.6; 48.12), he tells how the Christ he encountered in a vision announced: 'I am the Alpha and the Omega, the first and the last, the beginning and the end' (Apoc 22.13; cf. 1.17; 2.8). He means that just as the whole of creation is to culminate and find its completion in Christ, the Omega, so also the whole of creation had its beginning in him, the Alpha of God's creation. The pre-existent Christ was the principle behind God's creation. In another expression, its foundation: 'for no other foundation can any one lay than that which is laid, which is Jesus Christ' (1 Cor 3.11).

Again, in an effort to render more precise the active role in creation that they believed Christ to have played – following up the hints dropped in the Old Testament concerning the creative function of Wisdom – the New Testament writers employ a number of prepositions which express the intimate link between Christ and what is created. It is true that in the Letter to the Hebrews the direct creative activity which in the Old Testament was ascribed to God is ascribed without more ado to Christ:

> Thou, Lord, didst found the earth in the beginning,
> and the heavens are the work of thy hands;
> they will perish, but thou remainest;
> they will all grow old like a garment,
> like a mantle thou wilt roll them up,
> and they will be changed.
> But thou art the same,
> and thy years will never end (Heb 1.10-12; cf. Ps 102.25-27).

But more often creation is said to have taken place *through* Christ: 'all things were made *through* him, and without him was not anything made that was made' (Jn 1.3). 'The world was made *through* him' (Jn 1.10), says St John; and the Letter to the Hebrews begins with the encouraging message that God 'in these last days... has spoken to us by a Son, whom he appointed the heir of all things [= the Omega], *through* whom also he created the world' (Heb 1.2). To 'through' St Paul adds 'in':

> For *in* him all things were created, in heaven and on
> earth, visible and invisible, whether thrones or do-
> minions or principalities or authorities – all things
> were created *through* him and for him (Col 1.16).

And creation *through* or *in* Christ is seen not merely as
some past event, but also as an abiding reality in the
present state of creation. Christ still exercises his power
over creation: he is 'upholding the universe by his word
of power' (Heb 1.3); it is Christ 'for whom and by whom
all things exist' (Heb 2.10); or, as St Paul puts it, 'in him
all things hold together' (Col 1.17). If there is one passage
which best expresses, in an almost credal confession, Paul's
mind on the subject of the connection between Christ
and creation, it must be the following:

> For although there may be so-called gods in heaven
> and on earth – as indeed there are many 'gods' and
> many 'lords' – yet for us there is one God, the
> Father, from whom are all things and for whom we
> exist, and one Lord, Jesus Christ, through whom
> are all things and through whom we exist (1 Cor
> 8.5f.).

Christ and eternity

In view of the remarkable extent of the evidence in the
New Testament which links Christ both originally and
continually with created reality, it is strange that this
revealed truth plays so small a part in the doctrine of the
Church. Indeed, it would be no exaggeration to claim that
the truth, to which so many statements in the New
Testament lend support, is quite unfamiliar to most

Christian believers. But before mention is made of the reasons why such a key truth seems to have been allowed to lie largely forgotten, it will be best to complete the review of the relevant New Testament ways of expressing the truth of this mystery. Obviously, the root difficulty with the mystery lies in the need it imposes of supposing that Christ actually existed in order to be able to take his part in the divine work of creation. It is, to say the least, unusual to have to imagine the historical Christ somehow or other existing before the beginning of history. But further statements from the New Testament may show the way towards the divining of what is meant by the positing of this curious state of affairs.

To a certain unavoidable extent the quotation from the New Testament of those passages and sentences which show Christ to be involved, somehow, in the creative activity of God has done violence to the New Testament theology of creation – the way in which New Testament writers have tried to express, with such means as they had available, their new, Christian faith in creation. In order to bring out the range and force of the evidence, Christ's role in creation has been – rather misleadingly – isolated from his role in the world's salvation. Just as has been shown in the case of the Old Testament writers, where faith in creation followed on and grew out of their convictions concerning God's overall saving power, so also in the New Testament writers: their faith in Christ's creative role grew out of their complete conviction concerning his overall salvific mission. It is because Christ is the world's saviour that he came to be believed as having also a part in the world's very creation. The means of expressing this important belief were to hand – the figure of Wisdom and her role in God's creation. But in order to apply the necessary corrective to what has been forced isolation of Christ's creative role, it must be shown how the New Testament writers expressed their fundamental belief in Christ as the eternally appointed Saviour of the world. The 'pre-existence' of Christ as operative in the world's creation must be seen as already involved in his 'pre-destination' by God as that same world's saviour.

It is perhaps St Peter who best states the simple fact of Christ's predestination: 'he was destined before the foundation of the world but was made manifest at the end of the times for your sake' (1 Pet 1.20). The preceding verse, with its mention of 'the precious blood of Christ, like that of a lamb without blemish or spot', makes it clear that it is as *Saviour* that Christ is pre-destined from before creation. His appearance in our human history, at the point where the final age of the world begins, is considered as a manifestation of God's eternal Christ on behalf of mankind. In St Peter's statement there is clearly distinguished the eternal Christ from his (for us) later historical appearance. But St Paul, too, teaches the same truth by reminding his Ephesian readers how God the Father has eternally known and blessed them in his eternal Christ:

Blessed be the God and Father of our Lord Jesus Christ, who *has blessed us in Christ* with every spiritual blessing *in the heavenly places*, even as he *chose us in him before the foundation of the world*, that we should be blameless and holy before him. He *destined us in love to be his sons through Jesus Christ*, according to the purpose of his will, to the praise of his glorious grace which he freely bestowed on us in the Beloved... For he has made known to us in all wisdom and insight the mystery of his will, according to his purpose which he *set forth in Christ* as a plan for the fullness of time, to unite all things in him, things in heaven and things on earth. *In him,* according to the purpose of him who accomplishes all things according to the counsel of his will, we who first hoped in Christ *have been destined and appointed to live* for the praise of his glory (Eph 1.3-6, 9-12).

It is worthwhile dwelling for a moment on the kind of theological thinking about salvation which forms the background of this passage. The thought is of an eternal Christ. This eternal Christ represents God's whole plan, God's entire purpose, what God eternally wills to accomplish and effect through his action in the world. St Paul's insight consists in seeing the utterly basic truth contained in faith in Christ: that Christ is precisely that which God eternally has in mind. Christ is what God primarily and eternally wills. In Christ, for Paul, is revealed the ultimate mystery of God's will with regard to what God creates – men most especially, of course, but also the whole of reality, which is created for the sake of men. Key, then, to the understanding of the passage from the Letter to the Ephesians is the pre-eminence of God's eternal will and purpose.

It is, after all, God's eternal pleasure, God's sovereign and independent will, and the eternal purpose and plan of that will in man's regard which must provide the relevant starting-point for an appreciation of the truths of the faith. Faith and theology need continually to recall that their terms of reference are what in fact God eternally and freely *chose* to reveal of himself and his purposes. Old Testament writers had no hesitation in stressing the pre-eminence of God's will (Job 23.13; Ps 115.3; 135.3-6; Ecclus 33.13) with its unshakeable purpose (Is 14.24-27; 46.9-11; Prov 19.21) and hidden plan which was revealed through the prophets (Deut 29.29; Amos 3.7; Dan 2.47). But it is St Paul who is most acutely conscious that his role as minister of 'the word of truth, the gospel of your salvation' (Eph 1.13) involved him in the work of revealing and proclaiming God's eternal plan, 'the mystery of the gospel' (Eph 6.19). As he told the Corinthians, with more than a hint – as has been seen above – at Christ:

We impart a secret and hidden wisdom of God, which God decreed before the ages for our glori- fication. None of the rulers of this age understood this, for if they had, they would not have crucified the Lord of glory. But, as it is written, 'What no eye has seen, nor ear heard, nor the heart of man conceived, what God has prepared for those who love him', God has revealed to us through the Spirit... And we impart this..., interpreting spiritual truths to those who possess the Spirit (1 Cor 2.7-10, 13).

His claim to be heard rested on this: 'This is how one should regard us, as servants of Christ and stewards of the mysteries of God' (1 Cor 4.1). He had knowledge of mysteries to impart: 'I became a minister according to the divine office that was given me for you, to make the word of God fully known, the mystery hidden for ages and generations but now made manifest to his saints' (Col 1.25-26). This knowledge was of God's mysterious will: 'We have not ceased to pray for you, asking that you be filled with the knowledge of his will in all spiritual wisdom and understanding' (Col 1.9).

But for Paul the mysterious will of God is, concretely, Christ himself: 'To [the saints] God chose to make known how great among the Gentiles are the riches of the glory of this mystery, which is Christ in you, the hope of glory' (Col 1.27). The Colossians were 'to have all the riches of assured understanding and the knowledge of God's mystery, of Christ, in whom are hid all the treasures of wisdom and knowledge' (Col 2.2-3). Paul wrote of 'how the mystery was made known to me by revelation', so that his Ephesian readers 'can perceive my insight into the mystery of Christ, which was not made known to the sons of men in other generations as it has now been revealed to his holy apostles and prophets by the Spirit' (Eph 3.3-5). The Colossians were to pray 'that God may open to us a door for the word, to declare the mystery of Christ... that I may make it clear, as I ought to speak' (Col 4.3-4), because, as Paul explained to the Ephesians, 'to me, though I am the very least of all the saints, this grace was given, to preach to the Gentiles the unsearchable riches of Christ, and to make all men see what is the plan of the mystery hidden for ages in God who created all things' (Eph 3.8-9).

Christ and creation

'The plan of the mystery hidden for ages in God who created all things' – the phrase, perhaps better than any other, sums up Paul's view of Christ as the pre-existent and predestined principle behind all God's action: what

God eternally has in mind and will, the essentially mysterious plan and purpose that he is revealing and realizing in history. The phrase also shows the vitally close connection between the plan which God has eternally in mind to fulfil – his salvific purpose in Christ towards all reality – and his original, free decision to create reality outside himself. God creates all things originally because he plans to save and fulfil them in Christ. Thus Christ is the principle involved in the very creation of reality, as well as being the saviour of all that is created. And this because Christ is what God envisages eternally in planning and willing his whole activity. Further, the phrase brings the attention back to the passage from the Letter to the Ephesians which was quoted above. St Paul views himself and his readers in the light and context of God's eternal and mysterious design which is Christ. He sees how in the eternal Christ, predestined by God in his eternal planning, to be the world's salvation, each individual Christian is also predestined – intended by God for no other purpose than to be part of the fulfilment of his own eternal purpose, which is, mysteriously, nothing else than Christ. It is to become partakers in the personal mystery of Christ – 'to be his sons through Jesus Christ' – that God, in his love, has eternally predestined men to be Christians, and therefore, for the same reason also, originally creates them. Creation and salvation are thus, to Paul's mind, two aspects of the one activity of God which has Christ alone as its eternal guiding principle.

There is a single, neat statement of St Paul which brings out the whole unity of God's activity: 'for we are [God's] workmanship, *created in Christ for good works*, which God prepared beforehand, that we should walk in them'

(Eph 2.10). And the idea that God eternally intends men for the real fulfilment which is to be found only in Christ, and therefore creates solely with Christ eternally in mind, is expressed in a number of places in the New Testament. Thus in the apocalyptic account of the Last Judgment it is related how 'the King will say to those at his right hand, "Come, O blessed of my Father, inherit the kingdom prepared for you from the foundation of the world"' (Mt 25.34) – a message which is substantially the same as St Paul's at the beginning of the Letter to the Ephesians. The same message, that men are 'chosen and destined by God the Father and sanctified by the Spirit for obedience to Jesus Christ' (1 Pet 1.2), is contained in the metaphor, again familiar enough to most Christians, of the book of life; damnation will come upon 'every one whose name has not been written before the foundation of the world in the book of life of the Lamb that was slain' (Apoc 13.8; cf. 17.8). But more expressly in St Paul's teaching about God's foreknowledge of men and its purpose:

We know that in everything God works for good with those who love him, who are called *according to his purpose*. For those whom he foreknew *he also predestined to be conformed to the image of his Son*, in order that he might be the first-born among many brethren. And those whom he predestined he also called; and those whom he called he also justified; and those whom he justified he also sanctified (Rom 8.28-30; cf. 11.2).

God's *fore*knowledge of men, his knowledge of them from the divine point of view of eternity, is a knowledge in which he sees men as predestined eternally to belong to Christ – 'to be conformed to the image of his Son'. God's knowledge of the eternal Christ is of Christ as 'the first-born among many brethren'. God sees men, in other words, in terms of Christ, in terms of him who is the divine but still fully human prototype of mankind, and in whom men are to find their true humanity. The calling, justifying and sanctifying of men are divine works which are, so to speak, subsequent on God's choice of them in Christ, the predestination and creation of them in the eternal Christ. God's whole work of the creation and sanctification – or salvation – of what is outside of himself is thus done in terms of Christ.

The new creation

It is instructive to see how, in the New Testament, creation and salvation are so closely associated that salvation is frequently looked upon as a renewal of the original creation. In fact, the salvation of the world which has been begun through the coming of Christ into the world and through the subsequent outpouring of Christ's Spirit upon all flesh (cf. Acts 2.16-21), and which is still to be brought to its fulfilment in the fulness of time, is simply described as 'a new creation' (Gal 6.15).

'The form of this world is passing away' (1 Cor 7.31). This fact is of importance for a correct attitude to the world in which life is still lived:

> I consider that the sufferings of this present time are not worth comparing with the glory that is to be revealed to us. For the creation waits with eager longing for the revealing of the sons of God; for the creation was subjected to futility, not of its own will but by the will of him who subjected it in hope;

because the creation itself will be set free from its bondage to decay and obtain the glorious liberty of the children of God. We know that the whole creation has been groaning in travail until now; and not only the creation, but we ourselves, who have the first fruits of the Spirit, groan inwardly as we wait for adoption as sons, the redemption of our bodies (Rom 8.18-23).

The whole creation, man and man's whole world, now stands to be created anew through the saving action of God the Father, who adopts men as his sons through the gift of the Holy Spirit of his Son.

This fatherly, saving gift of the Spirit of sonship comes to men in baptism and endows them with a new personality, that of the Only-Begotten Son himself, Christ our Lord: 'For as many of you as were baptized into Christ have put on Christ' (Gal 3.27). Our old selves undergo *a re-creation*:

Put off your old nature which belongs to your former manner of life and is corrupt through deceitful lusts, and be renewed in the spirit of your minds, and put on the new nature, *created* after the likeness of God in true righteousness and holiness (Eph 4.22f.).

This is a fact which sets new standards of behaviour: 'Do not lie to one another, seeing that you have put off the old nature with its practices and have put on the new nature, which is being renewed in knowledge after the image of its creator' (Col 3.9f.). Being a Christian, being saved, involves the re-creation of man's creaturely existence: 'if anyone is in Christ, he is a *new creation*; the old has passed away, behold, the new has come' (2 Cor 5.17).

64

God's saving purpose in sending his Son is that Christ the Son 'might *create* in himself one new man' (Eph 2.15.) This new and final creation is prefigured in God's creation of the first man. The new man is the spiritual, heavenly counterpart and surpassing fulfilment of Adam:

> Thus it is written, 'the first man Adam became a living being'; the last Adam became a life-giving spirit. But it is not the spiritual which came first but the physical, and then the spiritual. The first man was from the earth, a man of dust; the second man is from heaven. As was the man of dust, so are those who are of dust; and as the man of heaven, so are those who are of heaven. Just as we have borne the image of the man of dust, we shall also bear the image of the man of heaven (1 Cor 15.45-49).

Thus, to come to a fuller understanding of the saving work of Christ for the world and for man, it is necessary to see that the work of re-creating man in the image and likeness of Christ is considered in the New Testament as a repetition and at the same time as a surpassing and perfecting of God's original creation of the first man. That first creation is the model for God's new creation of man in Christ. Adam 'was a type of the one who was to come' (Rom 5.14). Yet the difference between the two creations – Paul contrasts them in terms of Adam and Christ – and their effects on us must also be marked: 'as in Adam all die, so also in Christ shall all be made alive' (1 Cor 15.22). The first creation of man who sinned left all men sinners doomed to die: 'sin came into the world through one man and death through sin, and so death spread to all men because all men sinned' (Rom 5.12).

The second creation, the saving re-creation in Christ, justifies men before God and gives them a holiness of life which derives from him who is God in person:

> For if many died through one man's trespass, much more have the grace of God and the free gift in the grace of that one man Jesus Christ abounded for many. And the free gift is not like the effect of that one man's sin. For the judgment following one trespass brought condemnation, but the free gift following many trespasses brings justification. If, because of one man's trespass, death reigned through that one man, much more will those who receive the abundance of grace and the free gift of righteousness reign in life through the one man Jesus Christ. Then as one man's trespass led to condemnation for all men, so one man's act of righteousness leads to acquittal and life for all men. For as by one man's disobedience many were made sinners, so by one man's obedience many will be made righteous (Rom 5.15-19).

The parallelism in which St Paul can speak of Adam and Christ rests on an understanding of Christ's work of re-creation in terms of God's first creative work. As truly as our re-creation in Christ surpasses and fulfils our original creation, so does our original creation provide the model and type for the understanding of our re-creation.

On a cosmic scale the New Testament looks forward to the re-creation of the whole of created reality: 'according to his promise we wait for new heavens and a new earth in which righteousness dwells' (2 Pet 3.13). In a vision St John imagined the coming of creation's renewal for which all of us still wait:

> Then I saw a new heaven and a new earth; for the
> first heaven and the first earth had passed away,
> and the sea was no more. And I saw the holy city,
> new Jerusalem, coming down out of heaven from
> God, prepared as a bride adorned for her husband;
> and I heard a great voice from the throne saying,
> 'Behold the dwelling of God is with men. He will
> dwell with them and they shall be his people, and
> God himself will be with them; he will wipe away
> every tear from their eyes, and death shall be no
> more, neither shall there be mourning nor crying
> nor pain any more, for the former things have passed
> away'. And he who sat upon the throne said
> 'Behold, I make all things new.' (Apoc 21.1-5).

In considering salvation in terms of the renewal of the
original creation the New Testament was, once again,
following the lead of the Old. There the promise of cosmic
renewal had been held out to the generations yet to come
– a new creation performed by God to replace the old:

> For behold, I create new heavens and a new earth;
> and the former things shall not be remembered
> or come into mind.
> But be glad and rejoice for ever
> in that which I create;
> for behold, I create Jerusalem a rejoicing,
> and her people a joy (Is 65.17f.).

God will so satisfy all the needs of his people, so fulfil
all their desires, that he must be said to *re-create* the world
as that people knew it:

> When the poor and needy seek water, and there is
>   none,

and their tongue is parched with thirst,
I the Lord will answer them,
I the God of Israel will not forsake them.
I will open rivers on the bare heights,
and fountains in the midst of the valleys;
I will make the wilderness a pool of water,
and the dry land springs of water.
I will put in the wilderness the cedar,
the acacia, the myrtle, and the olive;
I will set in the desert the cypress,
the plane and the pine together;
that men may see and know,
may consider and understand together,
that the hand of the Lord has done this,
the Holy One of Israel has created it (Is 41.17-20).

Not that the cosmic renewal, the world's re-creation, will be only external. On the contrary, it is man's inner holiness that is God's most important re-creation:

Shower, O heavens, from above,
and let the skies rain down righteousness;
let the earth open, that salvation may sprout forth,
and let it cause righteousness to spring up also;
I the Lord have created it (Is 45.8).

God's saving work is to be the answer to the Psalmist's prayer that God might create in him a clean heart, a new and right spirit within him (Ps 51.10):

A new heart I will give you, and a new spirit I will put within you; and I will take out of your flesh the heart of stone and give you a heart of flesh. I will put my spirit within you... (Ezek 36.26f.; cf. 11.19).

Both Testaments, then, consider God's saving action in terms of his creative action. Salvation can be looked at as a re-enactment of creation, a re-creation. Salvation in Christ is both promised in the Old Testament and expressed in the New as the new creation of man and his world at the hands of God. So if the biblical evidence is to be taken seriously, and especially that of the New Testament, both salvation and creation should be considered in terms of an eternal Christ who is the Father's working plan and purpose for the whole of the reality which he creates beyond himself. The creation of that reality is performed through Christ, and the reality exists, and remains existing, in dependence on Christ. The salvation or re-creation of man, for whom the rest of created reality exists, also depends on God's predestination of man in his eternal Christ. While it is impossible for the human mind to grasp clearly the whole sweep of God's eternal purpose in Christ from the divine and eternal point of view, it is possible, if the scriptural evidence is read aright and properly evaluated, to come to share something of the divine vision which is normative for the reality which entirely and continuously depends on God working through his Christ.

At the beginning of this chapter it was said that the chapter's purpose was to expound the theology of creation that is to be found in the biblical writers. In so far as this theology has been expounded above, it might be fairly said to fall short of that conceptual exactitude which must be the job of theology to achieve in its reflections on the data of the faith. Such a shortcoming must be certainly admitted. But it must also be pointed out that it would be grossly unhistorical to demand or expect from the biblical writers that clarity of conceptualization which can come only with the application of philosophical methods and terms to the revealed subject matter of theology. The biblical writers were no philosophers. Their aim was not intellectual consistency. They were, above all else, inspired and zealous preachers of the new truth about God and his ways that was revealed to them in Christ their Lord. If that truth was expressed in terms which seem to modern minds to be largely imaginative, and even crudely pictorial – terms, for instance, such as 'the pre-existence of Christ' – this is cause neither for surprise nor for rejection. It still remains the necessary task of the modern theologian to try and clarify the meaning of the undoubted, if clumsy, teaching of the New Testament concerning the link between Christ and God's whole salvific, and therefore *also* creative, activity.

CHAPTER 4

THE CHRISTIAN THEOLOGY OF CREATION

If it is so clearly the case that in the Christian scriptures creation is revealed as a Christian mystery, to be seen in the light of Christ and inextricably bound up with, and needed for the full understanding and appreciation of, Christian salvation, then it might fairly be asked why such a truth has remained so neglected by so many great theologians. Should it have been left to a scientific Christian visionary like Teilhard de Chardin to reinstate the Christian meaning of creation and the evolutionary processes involved in its development? Whatever happened to the Christian theology of creation between St Paul and Teilhard? It will be useful to suggest some reason why this vital part of Christian theology has remained relatively rudimentary, and to point to some ways in which the truth of creation may be better appreciated.

Some reasons for neglect

Teilhard himself, speaking of the Omega point, admitted that

> doubtless I should never have ventured to envisage it, or formulate the hypothesis rationally if, in my consciousness as a believer, I had not found not only its speculative model but also its living reality (*The Phenomenon of Man*, London 1965, p. 322).

Even if it is admitted that Teilhard was a man of outstanding religious gifts, deeply conscious of the living reality of Christ in the creation around him, it remains strange that so many others seem to have achieved so little of the same consciousness, even though they shared the same Christian faith. There are signs that modern Christian theology, especially under the influence of the great Protestant divine, Karl Barth, is bringing back to the Christian consciousness the truth that creation is a basically Christian mystery: that, as Hans Küng has said,

> Jesus Christ... constitutes according to Scripture, the origin and foundation of being, the archetype and prototype, the light and power, the meaning and the value, the support and the purpose of creation (*Justification*, London 1964, p. 130).

But, as Küng goes on to remark:

> ...the chapter in the history of dogma dealing with this truth of faith remains to be written. It will turn out to be an important history of development, but probably also one of forgetting. It is not that this truth of faith absolutely disappeared but that it did not always remain in the forefront of consciousness (*ibid.*, p. 132).

Is it possible to suggest reasons why the Christian truth of creation went underground?

Certainly one of the reasons was that in the fourth century, at the time when the Arian heresy was abroad in the Church, it came to be thought that too close a link between Christ and creation involved the risk of Christ himself being included in the number of God's creatures. When it was essential for the survival of Christian orthodoxy that the full personal divinity of Christ should be defended and proclaimed, it could have seemed to have been playing into the hands of the heretic Arians if it were too crudely asserted that Christ is 'the first-born of all creation' (Col 1.15). Would it not look as though Christ were simply to be numbered among God's creatures? The Arians were satisfied to hold that Christ was a creature, even that he was the perfect creature. There was no need for him to be divine. Orthodoxy, under the vigorous leadership of the much persecuted Athanasius, saw that if Christ were not personally divine then he could not have personally worked the reconciliation between God and man which is man's salvation. But it was obviously not a time in which it was convenient to pursue theological speculation concerning Christ's role in creation – a role which might appear to give him only a subordinate status with God, and so make him less than divine. Earlier theologians, in particular the second-century defenders of the Christian faith who are called the Apologists, had felt no such misgivings. They had been encouraged by Greek philosophical thinking to explain Christ's status with God in terms of his being eternally God's *Logos* – his Word or self-expression. When God creates he expresses himself in his creation. Naturally, then, his *eternal* self-expression, who is Christ, has a part to play in the *temporal* self-expression of God which is creation. Hence the role of Christ in creation was still an accepted part of the Christian revelation and figured widely in the theology of those times. But by the fourth century, for the reason indicated above, no theology which might seem to subordinate Christ to God could be safely developed. So the link between Christ and creation became weakened in the Christian consciousness.

Again, developments in the theology of the Trinity

moved away from earlier patterns where the distinction between the three Persons had been expressed in accordance with the different functions that Father, Son and Holy Spirit were thought to perform in the work of creation and salvation. By the fifth century interest centred more on the metaphysical unity of the Godhead and on how the Trinity of Persons could be reconciled with it. The theology of the Trinity became more a matter of philosophical reflection, and theologians sought for an internal or psychological 'explanation' of the mystery of the Three in One. As the focus of interest moved from the functions of God in action to the unity of his divine essence, so also interest in creation lapsed. It became simply a work of the one God *ad extra* (i.e., outside himself) without further elaboration. No special function was assigned to any of the three Persons, since this was thought to disrupt the oneness of the Creator. A passage from St Augustine will illustrate this trend:

> When we call both the Father 'the principle' and the Son 'the principle' we are not enumerating two creative principles; because the Father and the Son together form a single principle with regard to creation – single Creator just as they are a single God... It must be admitted that the Father and the Son are the principle of Holy Spirit, not two principles. But just as the Father and the Son are one God and, as far as concerns creation, a single Creator and a single Lord, so are they a single principle as far as the Holy Spirit is concerned. But with regard to creation the Father, the Son and the Holy Spirit form a single principle, just as they form a single Creator and a single Lord (*On the Trinity*,

5.13-15).

This kind of high theological thinking leaves little room for the revealed connection between Christ and creation. Of course, to speculate about the unity of the Godhead in its three-ness is a legitimate concern for the theologian. But it appears to be the case that theological speculation, pursued almost for its own sake, can leave the whole of the truth revealed in Christ defective and distorted. It is a matter of maintaining balance. Theories which lead to an unorthodox subordination of Christ are, as has been shown, dangerous in their consequences for Christian salvation. On the other hand, theories of the Godhead which fail to assign a central position in God's plan and work to Christ may also be misleading.

Yet the fashion for Trinitarian speculation – not without making real progress and bringing certain rewards – lasted long in the history of the Church's doctrine. Here is another example of the same approach to the theology of the Trinity with consequences for the doctrine of creation:

> Properly speaking, to create is to cause, i.e., to produce the existence of things. Now because every agent impresses its own likeness on what it effects, you can discover the principle of the action by looking at the effect of the action itself – so what produces fire is in fact fire. Thus creating belongs to God according to his existence (which is his very essence) – existence common to all three persons. Therefore creation is not an action which is proper to one definite Person, but is an action common to all the Trinity (Thomas Aquinas, *Summa Theologica*, 1.45.7).

The philosophical approach to creation inherent in this passage is quite justifiable in theology. It is necessary for the theologian to enquire about God in so far as he is the ultimate cause of existence. At the level of the sheer existence of things outside God there is no call for a differentiation between the Persons of the Trinity. God as the essentially existent, and so as the cause of all other existents, is a single principle. In considering God as a single principle, a single and essentially existing nature, personal distinctions do not apply. These distinctions arise when it is a question of the personal self-relatedness of God – of the God of Christian experience who is Father, Son and Spirit. So also with creation: if creation is considered solely at the level of the production of existents outside God, there is no need to assign any particular place to Christ in that divine activity. Only when creation is considered as part of the Christian revelation must a new and deeper idea of creation be presented by the theologian; and the idea must contain a basic reference to Christ. Unfortunately theology became accustomed to take the philosophical rather than the strictly Christian approach to creation, and the place of Christ in creation was left to one side.

The necessary point of view

But more telling than the risk of heresy or the use of perhaps over-philosophical approaches to the theology of the Trinity in the dropping of the Christian mystery of creation from the Christian consciousness has been the failure on the part of so many theologians to see God's

saving work as a whole. Frequently theological contro-
versy within the Church has blinkered the theologians
involved, so that their theological vision has been perforce
narrowed down to one area of dispute – that to do with
grace, for instance – and their feel for the unified range
of God's grace-full action in man's regard has been lost.
There is, then, an urgent need for the removal of blinkers
and the restoration of the ability to see the full scope and
depth of the divine work. The theological vision which
thought-out faith can afford must be widened; and this
calls for a readjustment in the way the mysteries of the
faith are to be viewed. To effect just such a readjustment
is surely the highest service that a theologian has to offer
the Church. It is his work to see that the faithful are
allowed to see – with the eyes of faith – the mysteries in
which they believe set out clearly and in their due propor-
tions and connections.

In order to correct the fragmentation of the Christian
faith into a set of fairly independent mysteries, some of
them seriously under-appreciated and others looming far
too large in the believer's consciousness – the Second
Coming, as well as creation, might serve as an example
of the former kind and the mystery of sin might be a good
example of the latter – the mysteries of the faith must be
held together in a single unifying perspective. But is such
a perspective either possible for, or available to, the
human mind? Is not such a perspective precisely the
perspective in which God himself can be said to view his
own action with regard to the world? And can such a
perspective ever be shared by man?

Yes: in fact man can share in the divine vision, the
divine perspective. It is the purpose of God's own reve-

lation of his plan for the world to enable man to share *by faith* God's own vision of that plan in its unity. Faith imparts to man a God-given glimpse of the mysterious and wonderful unity of God's design. Man can come to see that design from God's own point of view. Not, of course, with the directness of mental grasp which is God's own, but with such insight as God-given faith affords him – and with such a degree of human articulation as the science of theology can successfully elaborate. Man can be raised by God to a share in God's own eternal perspective – although, of course, man must be content to express what he is given to see from that eternal point of view in terms that remain crudely temporal and spatial.

If, then, the most is to be made of the share that God, in his revelation, would give man in his own view of his own unified activity in man's regard, creation must be seen in terms of man's salvation and fulfilment by God in Christ. By God's mercy and goodness it is in Christ that man is to be saved and ultimately fulfilled, as it is in Christ that man – and along with man the rest of man's world – is created. Christ is the Saviour of man in whose creation he already has a decisive hand. God's action in man's regard can be seen as having three major 'moments': creation, reconciliation and the final redemption and fulfilment of all things. Each of these three 'moments' takes place in and through Christ. The total action of man's God is Christoform. It starts with Christ, proceeds through Christ, and is completed in Christ. God's creating, reconciling and fulfilling activity hangs together round Christ. This is not to deny, of course, the possibility of a creation that neither envisaged nor depended on Christ. Such a creation would have been what might be called

the order of 'pure', that is, non-Christoform nature. But
this is not the actual order whose existence and Christo-
formity are revealed by God in Christ. The whole of
the real order in which man exists is Christoform – created
through, reconciled from its sinfulness by, finally to be
fulfilled in Christ. As St Paul says that 'God was in Christ
reconciling the world to himself' (2 Cor 5.19), so also God
is in Christ creating man and man's world, which stands
in time to be reconciled by, and at the end of time comes to
be consummated in, Christ. All the activity of God
envisages and takes place in and through Christ. In all
that concerns man God first has Christ in mind. Christ
is not an afterthought on the part of God. Christ is the
original and originating, mysterious but clearly, if par-
tially, revealed principle which lies behind all the aspects
of God's gracious, free activity towards man. In this
sense Christ is also the principle behind and operative
in creation. Creation is a Christian mystery, formally
distinct from, but not wholly independent of, the mystery
of man's reconciliation and final fulfilment in Christ.
Rather, creation in Christ underlies man's reconciliation
and fulfilment in him. Christ comes to save and fulfil what
is basically already his. This, very briefly, is how theologians should learn to express that share in the divine
perspective of eternity which is granted to all who believe
in the activity of God in Christ.

God's plan

The key to the shared vision lies in beginning the theological elaboration of the faith with the plan which God

in his eternity chooses to bring into full effect through the history of his created world. Certain modern theologians, like Karl Barth, place the eternal election of Christ by God, as the plan to be realised in history, at the head of all God's works, and so are able to assess those works in terms of that choice. The separable 'moments' of God's action are thus interrelated in the light of the eternal choice of Christ as God's principle of action in history. And in this way God's actions are not theologically elaborated – and not perhaps sometimes neglected – in distorting isolation. So God creates in order that, in accordance with his eternal purpose to be, in Christ, the God who reveals and communicates himself to man, he might have that to which he will in time reveal and communicate himself. As Hans Küng says in describing Barth's view:

> Barth considers creation the external reason for the covenant, and the covenant the inner reason for creation. The purpose and, therefore, the meaning of creation is the making possible of a history in which God will join with man in a covenant – and one which has its beginning, middle, and end in Jesus Christ (*Justification*, p. 14).

Creation is the way in which the history of God's saving of man, planned eternally in Christ, begins and is made possible. The eternal will of God to enter into covenant-relations with man in Christ is the internal reason for creation. After all, as Barth says:

> What God created when he created the world and man was not just any place, but that which was foreordained for the establishment and the history of the covenant, nor just any subject, but that

which was to become God's partner in the history, i.e., the nature which God in His grace willed to address and accept and the man predestined for his service. The fact that the covenant is the goal of creation is not something which is added later to the reality of the creature... It already characterises creation itself and as such, and therefore the being and existence of the creature. The covenant whose history had still to commence was the covenant which, as the goal appointed for creation and the creature, made creation necessary and possible, and determined and limited the creature (*op. cit.*, p. 21f.)

Creation is the first sign in time of God's eternal choice to be the saviour of man. Other express signs of God's choice will appear in the history of the chosen people, and above all in the historical incarnation of the eternal Son. But 'the ordaining of salvation for man and man for salvation is the original and basic will of God, the ground and purpose of his will as Creator' (*op. cit.*, p. 22).

A standing danger for theology is to forget that what it has to work on is a whole revelation which has its ultimate root in what God eternally wills to reveal, to impart, of himself. In the documents of the Second Vatican Council there are signs that the short-sightedness of the past is due for correction. It is encouraging to note passages such as the following:

By an utterly free and mysterious decree of his own wisdom and goodness, the eternal Father created the whole world. His plan was to dignify men with a participation of His own divine life. He did not abandon men after they had fallen in Adam, but ceaselessly offered them helps to salvation, in anticipation of Christ the Redeemer, 'who is the image of the invisible God, the firstborn of every creature' (Col 1.15). All the elect, before time began, the Father 'foreknew and predestined to become conformed to the image of his Son, that he should be the firstborn among many brethren' (Rom 8.29) (*Dogmatic Constitution on the Church*, 2).

Again:

In His goodness and wisdom, God chose to reveal Himself and to make known to us the hidden purpose of His will by which through Christ, the Word made flesh, man has access to the Father in the Holy Spirit and comes to share in the divine nature (*Dogmatic Constitution on Divine Revelation*, 2).

And again:

Through divine revelation, God chose to show forth and communicate Himself and the eternal decisions of His will regarding the salvation of men (*ibid.*, 6).

Not only does the restoration of true perspective into the believer's vision of the key mysteries of the faith make a coherent and credible pattern discernible in God's mighty action, but importantly, if almost incidentally, other mysteries can begin to be assessed in due proportion. Past imbalances in theology can be redressed. Thus sin is to be seen not as determining the whole of God's action with regard to man but, more justly, as a man-made obstacle to the fulfilment of God's loving design which makes the exercise of God's saving power all the more needed by man.

In the Middle Ages there was a dispute which helped to divide two schools of thought. It concerned the technical question of the motive of the incarnation. Why, or for what primary purpose, did the Word become man? On one side the Thomist school of thought replied that the motive was surely to redeem mankind from sin by dying on the Cross. On the other side the Scotist school said that this was not the primary motive, but that the Word would have become man whether man had sinned or not, whether he needed redemption from sin or not. It is by now an outmoded discussion. From a higher point of view than theologians of that time were prepared to take – from the point of view, that is, of God himself in his eternity, in so far as we are able to grasp it – it can be seen that God only ever had one plan and one purpose. God's plan eternally centres on Christ. All that God does outside himself is done in terms of Christ – whether it is the creation, the redemption or the completion and consummation of created reality. Christ is truly the Alpha and the Omega of God's intentions. Without denying in the least the sure doctrine that Christ died for our sins, it is still true that his incarnation did not depend on man's sin. God did not – in fact, could not – change his mind. It was his eternal intention that what he had created in Christ would come to its completion in Christ, and sin could not alter the eternal purpose of his love towards mankind in Christ. Human sin does not, as it were, call the tune to which God must dance. It represents a tragic attempt on man's part to find his own salvation outside the eternal purpose of God for him in Christ. As a fact of human history, it makes the saving intervention of God in Christ all the more necessary for man, if he is ever to reach the fulfilment planned eternally for him by God.

It is eternally God's will and purpose to save man irrespective of sin. Of course, in our present real order, salvation is *also* salvation from sin. But even if man had never sinned, he would still have needed saving, in the sense that man was never originally meant to achieve, without God's further personal intervention, that fulfilment which man is eternally planned and created by God to attain. The Christian revelation teaches that man is planned and created by God to be saved from his own inherent limitations through the God-given attainment of his share in the divine nature. Man's sin makes it impossible for man to accept God's gift of salvation. Sinful, as he is, he needs the healing gift of justification through faith and commitment to Christ before he is enabled, through this grace, to come to the fulfilment of that salvation which it is God's eternal plan to give him. Sin changes the way in which man, with God's help, is saved. It does not change God's eternal plan to save him. In preserving a point of view which does not lose sight of God's purpose from eternity, the mystery of sin is kept in proper perspective.

Human limitations

Of course, in the human effort to *express* the point of view which faith enables a man to share in his limited way with God himself, it becomes obvious that man remains at the mercy of his all-too-human powers of understanding and speech. In re-adjusting his mental sights in order to see the gracious unity of God's action which is spelled out in creation, salvation and the consummation of man and his world, man quickly finds that there are severe limits to the ways in which it is possible for him to express his faith's vision. Human language is built to express events and states that belong to a world of time and change. Although – mysteriously – God is not subject himself to time and change, man can think and speak of him and of his plan or purpose only as if he were subject to time and change. So, for instance, God can be thought of only as existing in the *time before* he created the universe. But God in fact exists in eternity, and in eternity there is no before and after anything. Similarly, God can be thought of only as deciding on a plan, or as expressing his purpose, at some fixed point within his eternity. But there can be no time-points in eternity. Eternity is not time which happens to lack both a beginning and an end. It is not time at all. So the state of God's affairs is simply not to be properly expressed in terms of time and of change. Just as there was for God no period of waiting before he created the universe, so also there can never have been for God a time when he was without his fully planned intention with regard to the universe he creates. For man, of course, the universe began a long time ago, and before that time there was no universe. Likewise for man God's plan for the created world has been realised and revealed in various historical stages, and its culmination is in the historically definitive incarnation and revelation of Christ. But man's time-ridden ways of thinking and speaking cannot adequately express the way in which God works of himself. God is, and so acts, eternally. His action involves no time, no change, no gradual revelation and realisation, for him; although it does so for man.

It is this fact that brings with it the need to speak, when trying to elucidate the Christian mystery of creation, of an eternal or pre-existent Christ. The idea of an eternal or pre-existent Christ obviously entails for the human mind certain insuperable difficulties. How can he who is a historical figure be said to exist eternally or 'before' the beginning of history? But the idea of a pre-existent Christ performs a function – essential, as has been shown in the previous chapter, for the fuller understanding of the Christian mystery of creation – in theology which it is important to try to understand. Christ is said to exist eternally, or to 'pre-exist' the creation of the world, insofar as it is he who is the sole pattern or plan in the divine mind for the divine activity involved in creation-salvation-consummation. It is not simply that the eternal Word or Son of the Father is said to pre-exist and to be that pattern. The pattern is the *incarnate*, fully human Word and Son who is *Christ*. It is towards him, and not towards some disembodied ideal, that God's activity looks from eternity. Created reality, and man especially, is eternally patterned on Christ. This is the basic truth that underlies the mentally frustrating conception of an eternal or pre-existent Christ. The conception is essential, however, if the fulness of Christian truth about creation is to be expounded.

It is true that the connection between Christ and creation must inevitably remain a mysterious truth to the human mind. This is because it is an attempt to express a vital truth about the action of God in creating reality outside himself; and the action of God can never be adequately or fully expressed in human concepts. Neither God nor his actions will be reduced to purely human categories. Only God himself can have a full grasp of his own being and his doing. Men must await his revelation, and that revelation can be embodied only in human terms. There must be, therefore, a shortfall between what man can either discover or even be told by God about God's self and his actions on the one hand, and God's self and actions in themselves on the other. Theology must try to bridge the gap and promote such understanding as is possible, with such means of conceptualization as are available. Where the refinements of human philosophy with its man-made clarity fail to promote that understanding, then the believing mind has to make do with the humanly more unrefined notions which are to be found in Scripture. The pre-existent Christ is just such a notion: philosophically impossible but theologically necessary. It is well to recall the words of St Paul:

> ...my speech and my message were not in plausible words of wisdom, but in demonstration of the Spirit and power, that your faith might not rest in the wisdom of men but in the power of God (1 Cor 2.4f.).

God's eternal purpose is not an impersonal plan which, while it may be divine in origin, does not really involve God himself. God eternally decides and plans to involve himself with man. He eternally chooses for himself self-involvement with man as man's salvation, to make himself the salvation of man, the God for man; and he commits himself in his eternity to being such a God. In other words, God chooses eternally to be, in the person of his only-begotten Son, Jesus Christ. God chooses to be a God who is so involved in man's salvation, so allied to man, as personally – in the person of his Son – to take humanity to himself and save and perfect and complete it, as Jesus Christ, God made man for the rest of mankind. Christ thus stands eternally first in God's loving purpose to be the God of the covenant with man. Of course as far as man is concerned, God's eternal purpose is at first only gradually revealed and fitfully realised in the historical relations between God and his chosen people in Old Testament times; and then definitively in the case of the historically incarnate and risen Son of God, Jesus Christ. For the final revelation and full realization of God's eternal purpose, in all its scope, man still waits, and will be waiting until the Second Coming at the end of human history. But God is not subject to human history, but Lord of it. Because man is tied to a historical view of things, he naturally tends to think of Christ as an after-thought on God's part; at worst as a sort of *deus ex machina* who came solely to save man from his sins. But Christ is what God eternally chooses to be, how God eternally sees himself in his Son – as incarnate Christ, who is man and the prototype and saviour of all men.

In speaking of the eternal or pre-existent Christ the theologian, following the inspired lead of Scripture, is trying to do his *human* best to express what God has revealed concerning the *divine* priorities in the plans for creation. Unavoidable though it is, it is of limited help to try to imagine a non-temporal pre-existence. The prefix 'pre-' cannot denote temporal pre-existence, since before time exists any form of temporal existence is ruled out. Rather, the prefix indicates a pre-temporal existence – better: a supra-temporal pre-eminence whereby Christ is believed to be present in the whole historical work of God's creation, reconciliation and fulfilment of the universe.

Conclusion

This chapter began with an account of the reasons why the Christian theology of creation has remained for many centuries strangely undeveloped. For the rest, the chapter has simply pointed out the lines along which the full theology of creation should develop in the Church. The path is not without its conceptual snags. But the theologian must seek out as adequate a conceptuality as possible for the better and fuller expression of his Christian faith. There is urgent need for a new theological appreciation of creation in Christian theology. Creation must be seen as an essential element in the total mystery of Christ. And that mystery can never be properly appreciated without taking creation into account.

In the light of the mystery of Christ and creation man can begin to glimpse his true reality, his real identity, which is in Christ. He can begin to appreciate the value of things created and redeemed in Christ; above all the value and meaning of human persons, created and saved from their own selfishness to partake in Christ's own eternal self-giving reality before the Father. A Christian doctrine of creation is indispensable for the understanding of the mystery of him who could say not only that he was for men the way, the truth and the life (Jn 14.6; cf. 1 Jn 4.9), the light (Jn 8.12; 9.5), the resurrection (11.25), the door (10.9), the bread (Jn 6.35,48,51), the vine (15.1,5), but more simply and significantly: 'I am He' (Jn 8.24,28,58; 13.19).

SELECT BIBLIOGRAPHY

As will be clear from the main contention of this essay, there is remarkably little written about the theology of creation. The massive treatment given to this topic in vol. III of Karl Barth's *Church Dogmatics* has not (yet?) found its way into more manageable books. But the following may prove helpful:

Piet Schoonenberg, S.J.: *Covenant and Creation*, (London: Sheed and Ward Stagbooks, 1968, p. b.).

Jean-François Bonnefoy, O.F.M.: *Christ and the Cosmos*, (Paterson, New Jersey: St Anthony Guild Press, 1965) [valuable for wide-ranging bibliography of Catholic works].

A. Hulsbosch: *God's Creation*, (London: Sheed and Ward Stagbooks, 1965, p. b.). [the first half of this book is quite helpful].

INDEX